The Book of Ariaa
Quotes for a Luminous Life

Ariaa Jaeger

Autographed copies of this book may be purchased at the author's website, www.Ariaa.com

ISBN: 978-0-9895503-5-2 (sc)
ISBN: 978-0-9895503-4-5 (e)
Visit my website: www.Ariaa.com
Printed in the United States of America
First Printing: November 2013
10 9 8 7 6 5 4 3 2 1

Other books by Ariaa Jaeger
"Ariaaisms ~ Spiritual Food for the Soul"
ISBN: 978-0-9895503-8-3 (sc)
ISBN: 978-0-9895503-3-8 (e)
Printed in the United States of America
Released September 2013

Table of Contents

Introduction

Quotes are like poetic affirmations, they are beautiful expressions of timeless wisdom which nourish and feed the spirit. They are concentrated tidbits of higher consciousness precisely poised to generate an optimal imprint in your heart. I love the way words move and dance across my computer screen as the infinite well within me moves like energy leaving a mark of love across the page. I have been inspired by the quotes of some of the greatest minds and yet I find within my own sanctuary, a vessel of unused words which when orchestrated together, bring forth the concert of my heart, the soliloquies of my soul.

As you read each quote, may they be a blessing to your heart, may the love I pour into these energetic verbal vibrations for the soul be felt to the depths of your being and touch you in guarded places, and open spaces yet unexplored.

With Beams of Love, Light and Laughter,
Ariaa

The Luminosity of
EVOLVING

"There is a horizon that by looking outside of yourself
you will never behold."

"Choose your friends wisely;
whatever you hang around with you become."

"There is a highest will for everyone's life
but you must choose to enter its door."

"Nothing undermines the soul more
than being untrue to who you are."

"There are no wrong or right paths
when searching for the light."

"A lighthouse often glows the brightest
when the storm brings forth the darkest clouds."

"Jealousy is a cancer growing in the small crevasses
where dissatisfaction thrives."

"Anger like alcohol strips away the veils
and reveals the core character of a human being."

"Any weakness whether emotional, physical
or spiritual leaves you vulnerable to the darkness
and can be used to undo you."

"Disagreements are a normal part of humanness
however there is an art to doing it effectively."

"Be aware of what you are giving allegiance to.
If you covet anything, covet love."

"Choose your battles wisely.
There is little on this planet
which can be accomplished through fighting."

"If you live inside the shouldn't
you'll never do the should."

"Discipline of the mind ignites rapture of the soul."

"There is no traffic on the road less traveled,
might want to head there."

"Do not be afraid of controversy for those whom it follows, change the world."

"Ego is nothing more than the obvious face of self-doubt; confidence is the face of self-love, self-worth and humility."

"If you want respect then lead by showing others respect."

"Lessons repeat themselves if you resist them and often they grow more intense which each return."

"Design a life where the color spectrum excludes the gray areas."

"Right now consider, if it does not resonate as truth it probably isn't."

"Life grows greater with each journey
on the road of an unexplored path."

"Living in fear is self-destructive and permanently
alters your brain chemistry."

"Love is the way of the peaceful warrior.
Love deflects evil."

"Dramas are a part of life…
they don't have to be a part of yours."

"Projecting your anger or emotions on others
crosses universal law and ensures returned karma."

"Love moves every mountain,
knowing calms every storm."

"Many people are in your life only for a season
but true friends will never abandon you;
their love like roots will continue to grow."

"Ego and confidence are exact opposites,
one comes from knowing, the other from not."

"Whatever you hang around with you become."

"No one can do anything to you unless you allow it."

"People treat you exactly the way you allow them to."

"Your vision only extends as far
as your imagination can take you."

"Reach out and connect with those who are different from you, for there is infinite wisdom in the unfamiliar."

"We cling to the familiar instead of reaching for the unknown where creation begins and limitation ends."

"The soul knows no color."

"Right now you are suppressing your emotions.
Find a constructive way to emote."

"Self-confidence and ego are exact opposites;
one comes from knowing, the other from not."

"The mirror of life is a constant reminder
to develop the higher self."

"When you strip away the facade
the purity of the soul shines through."

"The road less traveled is wider than you think,
might want to head there."

"The soul knows the path
the mind only sees the journey."

"There are no wrong or right paths when searching for the light for they all lead to the same divine door."

"Seeing through the pains of life,
embracing the bigger picture is one way
to transmute them into gentle lessons."

"We see in others a reflection of ourselves,
every person is a mirror to your soul
with rare exception."

"When you come to the edge of the mountain
your shadows will urge you to jump,
the angels will urge you to dance
but the still small voice within
will beckon you to fly."

"Those who see with their eyes behold the earth,
those who see with their hearts behold the universe."

"When you open the door of knowing
you unleash the kingdom within."

"You cannot develop the higher self
if you are always implementing the lower one."

"Your gut feeling is God speaking."

"Your values define your character and integrity.
Choose wisely."

"Traveling on unfamiliar roads
leads to new worlds unexplored, journey well."

"Whatever or whomever you contribute
your energies to, you are one with."

"You are more than you believe.
As more light comes in, your authentic self
is revealed."

"Whatever you dislike in others is mostly true of you."

The Luminosity of
TRANSFORMATION

"Common courtesy is the front door
to inviting angels in and opens new worlds
when extended to human beings."

"Your inner dialogue either raises
your spiritual frequency or it lowers it."

"The questions are as important as the answers."

"Even in your mistakes there is perfection."

"The only relationship which defines you
is the one you have with yourself."

"Mind over matter transforms the matter."

"Knowledge destroys innocence, wisdom feeds it."

"Doubt scatters faith and dissolves seeds of knowing."

"It is the wise soul who understands the phrase,
"this too will pass" because is always does."

"Karma is the universal law of cause and effect.
Whatsoever you think say or do will return to you
multiplied in one way or another."

"It is in serving that we are served,
it is in loving that we are loved,
it is in sharing pain and sorrow
that we develop our greatest compassion for others."

"A joyful life comes from unlearning
that which toxifies your heart
and feeding that which beautifies your soul."

"A victim mentality negates a victorious outcome."

"Be tender with the heart of man for mans' heart
has the blood of God flowing through it."

"The road to enlightenment begins
vvwith loving yourself."

"Crying over spilt milk will not refill your cup."

"Even in your darkest hour
you still have wings to fly."

"The lower worlds of demonics are real
and your actions, thoughts and deeds
either enable or deflect them."

"He who stands tall when the winds of change blow, scatters his seeds the farthest."

"Heartache can be liberating when you capture the realization of self."

"The greatest beauty emanates from those at peace with themselves."

"In all things, a leap of faith is the overture
to the symphony of soaring."

"The lessons we garner which drop us to our knees
are the ones which catapult us
to the highest plateaus."

"It is the wise soul who understands the mountain
is easier moved while still a mound."

"Personal pain can be transcended
when you discover it no longer serves you."

"Remain calm when the tide approaches
and the waters will transform you."

"Remove all beliefs which negate a universe of
limitless, infinite possibilities for only the ego denies
the existence of what the heart wishes to behold."

"Strip away the façade for there is freedom
in authenticity."

"The ego feasts on that which is worthless
while the soul feasts on that which is eternal."

"Those who live outside the parameters of fear
lead the most fulfilling and exciting lives."

"The sunshine appears when the rains
have thoroughly cleansed the soul."

"You can accomplish more in oneness
than you can in division."

"Transformation comes to those
whose hearts still yearn."

"Truth is like oxygen the more you inhale and exhale
it the healthier you look."

"When you remove the crust and the dust from
the human being the divine perfection stands forth."

"When you open the door of knowing
you unleash the kingdom within."

The Luminosity of
LOVE AND KINDNESS

"Kindness is like butter,
you can never have too much of it and it needs
to be generously spread on everything."

"Somewhere in the world someone is counting
their blessings and you are one of them."

"People respond to you in exactly the same way
as you feel about yourself."

"It is the wise soul who, upon acting,
asks the question, "Would I want it done to me?"

"Passion takes on many forms
and magnifies intention."

"Love is not an emotion,
it is the foundation of your existence;
love is not a feeling, it is a state of being."

"A heart full of love will never know a barren sunset."

"Soar beyond your own expectations
for a successful flight depends on your ability to
intertwine with those who already know how to fly."

"Behold the seed of LOVE, nurture it, prune it,
cling not unto it but release it to the wind
& you will populate the world."

"Being true to yourself is an asset,
being true to each other, a gift."

"I cannot explain the odd happenings of my heart
but love pours from it like crystal warm waters
drenching all those in my path."

"Diversity is to humanity what love is to the heart."

"Doing something nice for another
has lasting effects on your own soul."

"Friendship can be compared to an uncut diamond.
The more you shape and polish it
the more valuable it becomes."

"I would rather spend one year with an enemy
per chance to heal the strife than one hour
with a friend who has no integrity."

"Harness all the power of love within you
and you will light the entire universe."

"As humankind we have an obligation
to exercise the kind."

"Honor all elders for they were here before you
and have much to share."

"Clean out your spiritual closet
and restock your wardrobe with love."

"If you think of everyone in terms of "if they died
tomorrow," you will love them more today."

"I love not because I am human
but because I am divine."

"I shall not pass this way again
therefore let me leave love laden along the road."

"I would rather love you as a friend
than fight you as a lover."

"Love is a gift not an entitlement."

"Honor all elders for the wisdom that flows
through them is an endless wellspring
which irrigates all future generations."

"Love in all of its ecstasy and splendor is a wild beast
in its ardent bending of the heart."

"If you do one thing today, do this;
love with all your heart,
love with all your mind,
love with all your soul."

"Love is not the way you see things
it is the way you sense them."

"Kindness leaves an imprint upon the global heart."

"Immerse yourself in the dance, let it take you
into the abyss where magic unfolds
and miracles collide with reality."

"In the beginning there was the word
and the word was love."

"Look upon that which is good and right and true…
it will imprint on you."

"It is the wise soul who understands
the grains of life weigh more
when the river of love flows through them."

"Kindness is to the human spirit
what love is to the heart."

"Leave the door open to your heart,
only ghosts travel through closed doors."

"Let your cup overflow with love
and your table will always have guests."

"Life is far more enriching the more you connect."

"Love begets more love, laughter floods like rain;
passion fuels the fire and feeds the oneness flame."

"Love of the self is the genesis of all energy."

"The window to the soul is found
when the door to the heart is open."

"Love sees through the inertia of life
with vision so precise it always finds its target."

"See beyond all dogmas for there is only
one universal religion; love."

"Love seeks in search of nothing more
than a mirrored reflection of itself."

"My soul was created to praise,
my mind was created to create,
my heart was created to love,
my body was created and divinely designed to hug."

"No one ever leaves you...
they just continue their journey without you."

"Love is as an oak tree; it must root deeply to grow
yet sway gently to seed the winds."

"Perfect love does not measure, it sees only one."

"Repay darkness with light. Repay evil with goodness.
Repay hate with endless streams of love."

"Love is not the pathway it is the entire terrain."

"Right now you can love one another. Please do."

"Right now you can love yourself. Please do."

"Lose yourself in love, let it take you to places
you have never been before
and let it linger for a time."

"Souls often collide in unawaken remembrance
of yesterday's gone by."

"Love is the gateway to higher consciousness,
knowing unlocks the door."

"Spiritual growth is an act of expressing divine love
while procuring self-love."

"The differences which separate us all fall away
when you close your eyes and open your heart."

"Love is not a revolving door; it is a narrow passage
where every step journeyed synchronizes
the symmetry of two souls."

"The earth was created with a multitude of cultures
that ye may come to know yourself
through the eyes of others."

"The eye of love is pure and knows no race, no age,
no ethnicity and follows no agenda."

"The greater the love, the brighter the flame."

"The greatest love affair you will ever have
is with yourself."

"Love begets more love."

"The heart consumes what the eyes behold."

"Love does not always find a perfect fit,
it finds a place to nestle in the crevasses
where it can be nourished by shade and fed by light."

"The language of love transcends matter, overcomes
all fear and permeates every form of creation.
Where there is a heart of love,
there is a way unto all things."

"The love you give while on the earth lives
on long after you leave it."

"The price of endless giving, endless return."

"Let all things and all thoughts
emanate from a heart of love."

"The power of love is greater than the hate of man."

"The only unconquerable beast is the one
which refuses to let love in."

"Love which casts a wider net reaps
a grander bounty."

"The window to love opens
when the door to the heart is unlocked."

"The wonder of you comes to light
when the measure of you is love."

"Love is the consummate teacher, it bends you,
breaks you, twists you, tests you,
until it molds a rich palate of strength, resilience,
compassion, understanding and truth."

"There comes a moment in every life
when all that matters is love."

"You can be a cup of love or you can be the well."

"There is one thing that love cannot overcome...
neglect."

"Love is measured by the seeds you have sown
and the depth of those which rooted."

"Those who are intended to love you, will."

"Those who lift you in life need no name,
neither father, mother, sister or brother;
for the name of the kind heart is love."

"Today remember that love is manna for the soul
and the soul must be fed to thrive."

"Love does not decipher or rationalize,
it moves as energy, searching to find its matching
resonance then melds within its womb."

"Truth which cannot be seen with the eyes
is felt through the heart."

"Tune all your senses to love for there is no greater
power than the power that lies within."

"What matters most is what is inside your heart."

"Love will break your spirit, steal your soul and puncture your heart; love anyway."

"When love tries to show you the way, embrace it, for its wings are delicate and like a butterfly easily torn and the wind can easily steal it away."

"When you give your entire being over to love you raise the frequency of all living creation."

The Luminosity of
LIGHT AND ILLUMINATION

"Dysfunction is normal. Seek to be abnormal."

"It's not how high you go in knowledge,
it's how pure you are in spirit."

"Be kind and blessings will follow you."

"A heart which knows no boundaries
can fill the world with light."

"There is no identity,
only vibration beyond this universe."

"The light within the flame burns brightly
when the candle is in perfect balance."

"Awaken your awareness, give notice to the world
around you, hear the vastness of the universe
and lend an ear to its wisdom."

"You are a light, you decide if you are a bright light
or a dim one."

"Be aware of the shadow you cast upon humankind;
does it bring shade or does it prevent light?"

"Altered states of consciousness breed
higher states of being."

"Be kind to strangers, you never know what they
have overcome in their lifetime."

"Humility attracts light while arrogance deflects it."

"Cocoon yourself in love, rest within its hue, let it fill your every sense until the excess pours out on all."

"Great souls endure great trials
to reach great heights."

"Come into your inner temple and tune out the noise; where there is silence there is illumination."

"Each being was created with its own uniqueness
that ye may come to seek greater the one cord
within which likens you to all."

"Life is not about what you can get
it's about how much you can give."

"Everything is created perfect, you included.
All was perfect, all is perfect, and all
will forever be perfect, you just have to
step into sweet perfection and out of the illusion."

"Right now the high road is uncrowded,
might want to take it."

"Follow the light, you'll only get lost in the dark."

"I hold you in the light of perfection
until you see yourself in my reflection."

"We are all connected.
To help others raises your own sweet light."

"If light did not exist you would be enough
to illumine the entire universe."

"Keep shining your unique light for every ray
finds a pocket of darkness to illumine."

"Let my daily mindset be, "I am the infinite well
of the infinite spirit of the infinite light."

"If you look at the world, through the eyes of purity,
you rebirth your own innocence."

"Light is life; the paradox is that the darkness
needs light to thrive yet light needs mass to survive.
The one you feed, feeds all."

"Today remember to choose joy."

"Look closely and find the hidden blessings
in every situation, light is there no matter
how dark your hour may seem."

"Reach beyond the veils which blind you from the
light for the greatest fruits lay beyond the branches."

"If you want to get to the fruit of a tree
you have to go out on a limb; if you want to get
to the fruit of the soul you have to uncover
the roots and expose them to the light."

"Success is measured by the number of lives
you have touched not the number of dollars
in your bank account."

"Imagination gives flight to limitless worlds."

"The eyes behold the Light,
the heart beholds the Spirit,
the mind beholds the Oneness,
the soul beholds the Love."

"Inside every vessel is an infinite well."

"The light exists so it can illumine the darkness;
so it is with your soul."

"Light is the permeate force within all things.
Love is the quantitative force within all creation."

"The way of love is not through the heart
but through the light which illumines the soul."

"We are all connected, what you do affects everyone
around you, even the lives of total strangers."

"There is a highest will for everyone's life
but you must choose to enter its door."

"There is an ongoing battle for your soul,
feed the light."

"When the mind is open more light shines through."

"Those who dance in the light will always confound and confuse those who cannot dance at all."

"When the skies turn gray,
the wise will light the path with their inner glow."

The Luminosity of
SELFLESSNESS AND HUMILITY

"To touch the heart is beautiful
…to touch the soul …eternal."

"A single day of selfless giving can wash away
a hundred acts of selfishness."

"Today remember that if you are keeping score,
your gifts won't count."

"There is no reward for doing the right thing,
do it anyway."

"Allowing others to shine their light greater
illumines your own."

"Those who stand in your shadow
are the ones holding you up."

"Any man can make a baby but a real father teaches, nurtures, provides for and emotionally equips his child to become a productive citizen of the world."

"He who withholds finds a life devoid of charity."

"Let the whispers of the angels be adhered to in your heart that your path may be inviting and a blessing to other travelers."

"Today remember giving is its own reward."

"Plant one seed, populate your garden;
plant many seeds, populate the world;
plant without counting, you propagate
the entire universe."

"Serving others is an honor not a chore."

"The greatest measure of a life
is the ability to touch another."

"The purest souls are those who have little
but give it all."

"As day ends, I will search my soul in wonder,
did I give enough, did I love enough,
did the seeds I planted, flourish."

"The road you seed with kindness brings forth
the fruit of love."

"Today remember service without thought for self,
equals love."

"When you lift another up
you increase the value of your soul."

"Today remember higher consciousness begins
with the smallest acts of thoughtfulness."

"When man heals his ego
the world will know peace."

"Today remember that a life can be measured
by the goodness one enacts."

The Luminosity of
ANIMALS AND NATURE

"Greet the earth with a still mind and serene heart
and she will whisper to your soul."

"Those who see beauty in the world around them also
catch a glimmer of the beauty within themselves."

"The character of a human can be defined
by how he treats animals."

"All animals add to mother earth's ecosystem.
To kill them or to destroy their environment
is equivalent to destroying yourself."

"Be engulfed by nature, become one in the field
for every blade of grass is numbered in the sky and
every flower that blooms is there for your benefit."

"Every act of brutality whether to human or animal
defines the consciousness of the society in whole."

"When you stare into the eyes of an animal,
you see the soul of God."

"Get in touch with nature
and discover a kingdom of magic."

"Animals contribute to the light mass of earth
and should be considered
as valuable as any human being."

"Immerse yourself into the fold of everlasting love,
let the trees whisper to you,
let the leaves caress your flesh
and let the winds carry your song."

"Let that which exists in nature teach humankind
that all are one and all can co-exist in harmony
when you lead with love."

"See, smell, hear, taste and absorb the delectable
fruits of the earth. Give thanks for every sense you
have and everything that touches them."

"Love is the metamorphic spark within all creation
which unites all souls as one."

"Mother Earth is sacred and you are just her guest."

"Once you gaze the stars you cannot behold anything
but limitless possibilities."

"Run like the wind, let it dance through your hair,
for the earth longs to feel the divine rhythms
of your perfection."

"Spend time in nature
for it will teach you things man cannot."

"The rustling of change denotes the restlessness
of the world."

"Acts of nature are earth's way to rebirth and survive the damage imposed upon her by the uncaring few."

"There is symmetry in nature which also exists in you. Inner harmony is sustained by outer symmetry."

"When it comes to protecting animals
be loud and carry a passionate voice."

"When you feed an animal you feed your soul."

"The earth has messages that only the still can hear.
Be still."

The Luminosity of
JOY AND LIGHTNESS OF BEING

"Laughter is to the soul what breath is to the body."

"Just because it's the end of the road
doesn't mean it's the end of the journey."

"In life there are but two choices:
acquiesce or transcend."

"Be awake and the light will consume uncertainty."

"A smile can light up a room, warm a heart
or speak volumes in its radiance."

"A heart full of joy fills the world
with its own unique signature."

"Above all give others more than they expect
and do it with enthusiasm and joy."

"Celebrating the little things in life
will cause the big ones to come."

"Forgiving others is divine but forgiving yourself
is liberation squared."

"Joy begets more joy."

"When you let go there is abundant flow."

"Joy doesn't happen to you, it happens within you."

"Light the path with laughter
and the world is sure to follow."

"Live as if this were your last day,
laugh as if your life depended on it,
love as if there were no tomorrow,
surrender to the extraordinary
and you will behold fields of glory."

"Love seeds hope, hope seeds faith,
faith seeds gratitude, gratitude seeds joy."

"Perception is everything."

"Right now consider if it does not uplift, support, inspire, compliment or delight you, move on."

"Be joyful, for laughter leaves an echo
in the heart of humankind."

"Forgiveness is the doorway to the soul's liberation."

"Soul traveler, breathe deeply and allow what comes."

"The most peaceful heart is the one which knows
its limits and honors them."

"Right now you are contagious,
you are comprised of love, create an epidemic."

"Happiness does not depend on your
outer circumstances; it depends on your inner glow."

"You are more than you believe.
As more light comes in,
your authentic self is revealed."

The Luminosity of
BEING HUMAN

"Harboring unhealed emotions feeds
and creates physiological monsters."

"The art of making love is sacred.
Intimacy is a form of divine connection
coupled with divine expression
followed by divine release."

"The heart has answers the head can never conceive."

"Behold the wonders all around you,
for within each microcosm exists a new creation
waiting to be formed from your passion."

"Your body reveals what your mouth conceals."

"In your daily appearance,
you either reflect the extraordinary light of God
or the ordinary frequency of human emoting."

"A kiss is the signature of the heart
and conveys what words cannot."

"Believe only that which your senses reveal
for often the heart and mind are foe."

"Most humans utilize only a tenth of their brain.
Relocate yourself to the hundred percentile group."

"Do not drag your todays into your tomorrows
for each new day is a new beginning and the winds
of change blow with every sunrise."

"Never let your body dictate your mind
for your soul is timeless."

"Embrace your curves even if you are the only one
who does; when you become comfortable in your own
skin you unlock the doorway to your inner beauty."

"There is nothing quite as beautiful
as an emotionally healthy human being."

"To forgive others is divine
but to forgive yourself is liberation squared."

"Sexuality should be treated like an expensive
bottle of wine. You want to share it with somebody
special and savor every sip."

"Extremes create imbalance.
Imbalance creates extremes."

"Having more money will only make you more
of what you already are."

"You are either a liability or a blessing
to those in your life."

"Be at peace with all things great or small,
for rustlings draw the madness
and malcontent feeds the dark."

"Your body will tell what you inhale."

"Integrity is gauged best when no one is looking."

"Unless you set the parameters
others won't know when they have crossed the line
until they are already on the other side."

"Listening and hearing are two different things and
talking incessantly negates both."

"Much of what folks fight about, in the end,
rarely matters."

"You won't find God in the skies if you can't see God in each other's eyes."

"Physical strength is measured by what we can lift. Spiritual strength is measured by what we can bear."

"Prosperity is a state of mind and has little to do with materialism."

"Your mind is a powerful tool
which commands the body."

"Deal with your emotional pain
before it deals you ill health."

"When others show you who they are, trust it."

"Speak with your mind, not your lips,
speak with your heart, not your ego."

"The well-being of your consciousness
depends on those you listen to.
Distorted perceptions breed ugly infections."

"When you get defensive
you have already lost the battle."

"Think before you speak, act without delay,
love with pure abandon!"

"The stupidity of some leads to the compliance
in others."

"Those who scream the loudest
usually have the least to say."

"What you fail to define will define you."

"To skirt the edge of truth through evasion
is still lying."

"To think less of yourself is to think less of God."

"Understanding and compassion
are birthed from conflict."

"Walk upon the bridge of integrity,
meld into the crevasses of forthrightness
for your footprints leave a mold on all of life."

"The wonder of life is in the infinite ability
to intertwine."

"We are all human; imperfections lead to higher states of consciousness, to spiritual evolution."

"What others think about you does not define you, what you think about you, does."

"The body is a temple of the living God. How you adorn it is a direct reflection of the God that lives within you."

"When you open your heart you open your wings."

"The loveliest faces are seen with the heart
through the eyes of pure love."

"With every foul word you utter another angel
leaves your presence."

"Women come in all sizes, all shapes and all ages
so there is more variety."

"You are more relative than any microorganism
on the earth. You are the oxygen others draw from
when theirs has been depleted."

"Your affection is a reflection of your perfection."

"Your touch transfers what's in your heart."

"You are a complex creation worthy of self-discovery."

"When you let go of those in your life who no longer
add a spark of light to your spirit you make room
for those who ignite a blaze in your soul."

"What you inaccurately suspect in others
is usually more about you."

"God is in all things, it is man's ego that alters
the purity of his face."

The Luminosity of
INTENTION AND ATTRACTION

"Every thought, every action, everything you do
energetically affects everyone and everything
and reverberates throughout the universe
for eons to come."

"Before you act, ask yourself,
"Will it manifest?"
"Will it make a difference?"
"Will it come back to me multiplied?"
"Will it hurt anyone?"

"Make it your intent to be the light, to shine your
heart, to love without measuring the cost."

"A life achieves what the soul believes."

"Prayers ascend as energetic wings
and their migration manifests your reality."

"The universe knows you by your intent."

"A wish is a projectile energized by your intention and creates at the same magnitude as your intent."

"Bear witness to only that which feeds the soul, look upon only that you wish to embolden."

"Love is the lasting imprint you leave when you exit the room."

"Behold the vision and the means appears."

"Lift a silent voice unto the sky for that which remains unspoken becomes more energized by a wishful heart."

"By your definition of what is right and what is wrong will your character be formed and your karma ensured."

"Conceived in the mind, emboldened with passion,
empowered with knowing and fueled
with gratitude brings forth manifestation."

"Dreaming awakens the mystical
and brings to life the impossible."

"Fear is the great denominator between creating
what you want & drawing what you don't want."

"A heart captures and imprints what it dwells upon."

"If there is one seed of doubt within you,
the darkness will amplify it to create a toxic stew."

"There is no greater way to move a mountain
that to affirm it's already moved."

"If you don't want it, don't think it.
If you want it know it."

"Know that you know and then formulate your words
to follow suite."

"Learning to be a good receiver is as important
as being a generous giver."

"Let your lips bear witness to only that which feeds
the light for the food of evil is plentiful."

"All truth is divinely designed
to be completely transparent."

"Love is as vast as the color spectrum of the universe,
spackle the world with your own unique vibrancy."

"Make it your intent to be the light, to shine your heart, to love without measuring the cost."

"Negative thoughts, words and actions only hurt one person...you."

"Words leave a lasting mark on the heart and an imprint on the soul."

"Never build a wall you can't step over."

"One seed of doubt will grow an entire garden of weeds."

"Prayer is your direct line to the invisible to create the visible."

"The fire you feed assails long after it's out."

"Right now you are judging another human being.
Stop it."

"Right now you are judging yourself.
Stop it."

"If your heart is in the right place,
so shall the mountain be moved."

"What you think you are doing to another
you are in fact doing to yourself."

"Right now you can do a good deed
and never tell a soul."

"Set your standards high and the universe
will follow your lead."

"Speak with the mind what you want the universe
to hear for the lips profess the unknown
the soul professes the known."

"The eye captures what the heart beholds
and sears it to the soul."

"When man makes peace profitable
there will be peace."

"The universe does not judge you for what you
choose they only assist you in getting it."

"With every thought you underscore your reality."

"The universe revolves and evolves
through synchronistic knowing."

"The whispers of your heart speak louder
than your words."

"Love with such intensity that darkness fades to light."

"There must be a balance between giving and receiving;
if you give but never receive you attract need,
if you receive but never give, you attract loss."

"Thoughts and words leave a lasting imprint
upon the global consciousness."

"Today be aware of your thoughts, deeds and words,
for you can change the world one person at a time."

"What you do with your head is and earth thing
but what you do with your heart is a universal thing."

"What you see in others is true of you,
what you own in you becomes other's truth."

"What you love you magnify,
what you hate you draw, what you fear you amplify,
what you energize you attract."

"Whatever remains unhealed emotionally
will eventually manifest physically.

"The energy you pour into every action,
thought or desire continues to magnetically draw
like energy unto itself, amassing and growing
as it returns on the pathway of its origin."

"When loving people work together
to create a better world it alters the terrain."

"When you align yourself to love you can say
everything without speaking one word."

"When you free others to be all
they were created to be in your mind,
acceptance of yourself happens in your soul."

"Peace begets more peace."

"Wishing does not make it so...knowing does."

"Put a guard over your mouth
and only let intentional thoughts escape."

"You can accomplish more with silent though
than with the spoken word."

"Whatever you tell your mind
will become your truth multiplied."

"Your actions can be the difference in whether
you are a blessing or a liability."

"Your frequency is your shield,
raise it and your light deflects the negative.
Lower it and your light attracts the darkness."

"Your inner dialogue creates your outer reality."

"Your thoughts are a magnet to your reality."

"Honesty is more than just an occasional truth.
It is total sum of your character."

"I am the total sum of my thoughts,
every person in my life reflects my consciousness."

"Immersing yourself in the heavenly
transforms the earthly."

The Luminosity of
SILENCE AND SERENITY

"There is no better guru than the one
that resides within you."

"The sky lit up with wonder behold I bowed my head,
I heard the angel whisper, why seek ye the living
here amongst the dead?"

"Quiet is essential in reaching higher states of One.
There is power in silence and silence is power."

"Peace is a self-invoked state of being."

"There are tranquil waters beyond the surf
and there is power in navigating the breakers."

"Be good to yourself for you are a gift to all of life."

"There is wisdom in stillness...be still."

"Behold the color prisms of the soul
for you are a myriad of majesty."

"A house is not a home until the flames of passion fill it."

"Be good to yourself by allowing others
to be good to you."

"When answers can no longer be found outside,
divine solutions unfold inside."

"Be at peace and angels will adjoin you."

"Behold your heart soul traveler
for the memory of your sojourn
courses through your veins like the waters
of an endless flood drenching you with wisdom."

"Be insightful for there are worlds beyond
which only seekers find."

"Excessive emoting negates miracles."

"Extend yourself beyond your own limitations
for those who explore the soul discover the universe."

"He who spends time alone with himself discovers
the universe lives inside every cell."

"Home is not where you hang your hat,
it's where you hang your heart."

"In the stillness can be found Love in waves and beams, be still."

"Inner peace creates outer peace."

"It is within the silence of the soul that the voice of God echoes loudest."

"Mastering the art of self-sufficiency
empowers the human spirit."

"Behold the wonder of you coursing through
every vein, every pore, and every cell of your body.
Inside of you lives the unchartered Universe
waiting for the explorer to arrive."

"Shadows are cellular memories,
aspects of your lower self,
waiting to integrate in the fold of your higher self."

"Tenderness is a reflection of those at peace
with themselves."

"Emotionality is how we give things power;
staying centered is how we maintain core power."

"Enter the world with a holy presence,
be aware that all around you is a reflection of you
and is a perfect temple."

"Give pause when life doesn't go your way
for there is wisdom in the waiting."

"Let the sound of silence find you where the clamor of
the crowd cannot for there is wisdom in the silence."

The Luminosity of
GENUINE GRATITUDE

"Right now it is a choice; complain, criticize
and condemn or compliment and create."

"A grateful heart creates a domino effect
and generates greater good."

"Be thankful for and embrace the path of adversity
for it will lead you to enlightenments door."

"A thankful spirit creates immeasurable prosperity
and overflowing abundance."

"It is in the simple pleasures we often find
the greatest miracles."

"Be humble and you will behold the face of God."

"Let your heart be humble, your mind at peace
and let your lips be found giving thanks."

"Right now give of yourself, give of your time,
give of your money, give from your heart. Just give."

"The gift is only as good as the receiver."

"How can I see to my tomorrow's
if I fail to rejoice in my today's."

"Genuine gratitude renews the mind,
humbles the soul and awakens the heart."

The Luminosity of
TENACITY AND PERSEVERANCE

"There is nothing easy about the journey
of a thousand emotions which leads to the sphere
of serene splendor."

"The well within contains the waters
of infinite wisdom and never runs dry."

"Remember that life is the ultimate university
make sure you graduate with honors
both the bruises and the crowns."

"Loyalty can be defined as character in motion."

"The price is always higher where the pastures are greener and the fields are the most fertile."

"A heart on fire blazes trails the meek will never walk."

"Be mindful for the world around you is temporal
and all but love will fall away."

"Beauty is in the third eye of the beholder."

"Every conflict born of man stems
from an unyielding ego."

"Hate is a hungry beast and it grows
and feeds on energy. Don't give it yours."

"If I cannot kiss your lips I can at least kiss your soul.
If I cannot touch your flesh,
I can at least touch your spirit."

"I found the most beautiful place in the world;
it's in your eyes."

"It is in the whispers of the soul and the hunger of
the heart that compels the spirit to align itself to love."

"Be all you were created to be, soar to heights unseen
and let no man limit your range
for many have forgotten how to fly."

"It is rare when human beings actuate
and fully live their inherent divinity."

"Be not afraid of the storm,
for those who devour the blaze light the universe."

"It is the wise soul who understands that no matter
how hard you try, you will never fit in;
seek to stand out instead."

"Life is what you make it and if you don't extend
your awareness to other perimeters, you limit God."

"Live each day as if it were the last on earth.
Make yours a life of meaningful purpose."

"Open your heart to the needs of others
and yours too will be filled."

"Passion is a force of desire
which creates at the speed of light."

"If you want to dance in the rain
you have to be willing to get your feet wet."

"Right now you are the nourishment
an empty soul hungers for."

"Some people think it is passion which keeps the fire
lit when in fact it is passion which lights the fire."

"Those who stand the tallest in the saddle often experience the roughest ride."

"Do not be discouraged, it is often the last key of the bunch which opens the lock."

"You never know how high you can soar until you spread your wings."

"When you're in the middle of the fire,
dance upon the coals."

"Let your daily mantra be, "do it anyway."

"You never know what you can do until you have to."

The Luminosity of
PERSONAL EMPOWERMENT

"There are no greater answers than the ones
that lie inside of you."

"The climb that seems insurmountable is the one
which brings you to the greatest victory."

"Seek not to be validated, seek instead to be
comfortable in your own skin."

"The best way to ensure that no one pushes
your buttons is to eliminate the buttons."

"The beast will only harm you
if you perceive it as a beast."

"Self-denial is a landmine
which leads to eventual implosion."

"Be brave and your courage will shield you."

"A sense of self-rule can free a soul
while the need to control binds one."

"Be true to yourself and who you are,
don't let the actions of anyone define you."

"Do not let the negative emotions
of an unhealed person bleed out on you."

"If you want others to value what you do,
you have to first value you."

"You are your own shine;
no one can turn on the light within you but you."

"Self-expression runs akin to an artist laying paint upon a canvass. Master works occur."

The Luminosity of
FLOW AND FLUIDITY

"Ignorance is the root cause of hatefulness.
Don't be ignorant."

"I was given the gift of life;
it would be rude not to use it."

"Every moment counts and every count is momentous."

"Angels do not judge you for what you choose
they only assist you in getting it."

"Be flexible in life, bend with the flow of the winds
for Spirit speaks within them
and those who listen hear. Be still."

"Change is inevitable, inflexible is permanent."

"The roads of life may take many unexpected turns
but they always lead you home."

"The spectrum expands when the heart is open."

"When you bridge the gap between fear and
knowing, you surrender to the flow."

"You can move many mountains
but some are meant to fall."

"Discernment is a gift you give yourself."

"Do not to question when you don't get your way,
it may just be a blessing in disguise."

"Enjoy and be grateful for every moment
you create for they pass like rushing waters
into the sea of yesterday. Even if invisible, there is a
reason and season for every occurrence of your life."

"Free yourself from all limitations,
for they exist only in your mind."

"If it doesn't flow, let it go."

"In every life love must come and go,
it must ebb and flow, for it is in the waves
that seeds are scattered and it is in the still tide
that the roots burrow in."

"Let the dance consume you into the fold of life."

"Dreams are the universes way of speaking
and the higher self's way of hearing."

"Let the Divine flow of Spirit take you
where the ego cannot."

"Let the flow be with you."

"Life like doors must remain opened
if you truly wish to grow."

"Dreams are God's way of staying anonymous."

"Love keeps us flowing in perfect rhythms
to the Divine."

"Observe the world around you for far sweeter
is the life which beholds miracles in the ordinary."

"Fear is a dam which paralyzes divine flow."

"Sit up and take a genuine interest
in a fellow human being…
it may just be an archangel you are entertaining."

"Surrender in the face of adversity brings peace."

"There is a river known as life and those who flow
with the current find their ultimate destination."

"You can move many mountains
but some are meant to fall."

"When you let go there is abundant flow."

The Luminosity of
BEING AWAKEN AND AWARE

Be aware that a good life begins with a good attitude.

Be aware that a living with joy starts
with loving yourself.

Be aware of others around you
and consider walking in their shoes.

Be aware that an emotionally healthy you
is your best asset.

Be aware that living in fear will only draw
what you fear directly to you, heal your fear.

Be aware that self-pity alienates
your angels and guides.

Be aware that friends will come and go, let them.

Be aware that the universe is constantly listening
to your thoughts.

Be aware that your thoughts create your reality.

The Luminosity of
BECOMING AND BEING

Be a good listener and the light will lead you
through open doors and set you upon the waters calm.

Be at peace and angels will adjoin you.

Be awake and the light will consume uncertainty.

Be aware that you are the living experience
of the laws of cause and effect.

Be brave and your courage will shield you.

Be good to yourself for you are a gift to all of life.

Be insightful for there are worlds beyond which
only seekers find.

Be joyful, for laughter leaves an echo
in the heart of humankind.

Be kind and blessings will follow you.

Be kind to strangers, you never know
what they have overcome in their lifetime.

Be humble and you will behold the face of GOD.

Be mindful for the world around you is temporal
and all but LOVE will fall away.

Be silent and the stillness will transform you.

Be still and know; found in the vespers
is a treasure trove of knowledge.

Be thankful for and embrace the path of adversity
for it will lead you to enlightenments door.

Be tender with the heart of man for mans' heart
has the blood of God flowing through it.

The Luminosity of
CHOICE AND CHOOSING

Choose joy above all other emotions,
rise with a song in your heart and rejoice
in the music of your unique heart.

Choose to serve others and your cup will overflow
with blessings and bounty.

Choose to rise above the ordinary to blaze a trail
with extraordinary vision and actions.

Choose to walk away from that which no longer
serves you whether it be human, possessions,
old belief systems or emotional baggage.

Choose integrity over vacillations, stand for
something, and don't be afraid to live your truth.

Choose to do the right thing
even if it brings forth storms and rain,
even if you are the only one who does it.

Choose to love without withholding, give freely
to even the most unloving souls, for love, in the end,
always transforms you and the one you lavish it on.

The Luminosity of
THE "I AM" WITHIN

I am the sum total of my thoughts, every line
on my face reveals my emotional well-being.

I am the sum total of my thoughts,
every person in my life reflects my consciousness.

I am the sum total of my thoughts, every problem
I encounter I created as an opportunity to grow.

I am the sum total of my thoughts,
my health or lack of it reflects my beliefs.

I am the sum total of my thoughts,
what I feel is a result of my own understanding
and is no one else's fault.

I am the sum total of my thoughts,
what I think becomes my truth and I own it,
good, bad or indifferent.

Remember when your word was your honor?
It still is.

Remember when doing the right thing
was considered normal?
It still is.

Remember when your handshake and your word
of honor meant something?
They still do.

Remember when you could ask a stranger
who was hungry to come in and eat?
You still can.

Remember when gentlemen still stood up
when a lady entered the room?
Some still do.

Remember when good manners were revered?
They still are.

Remember when stargazing and catching fireflies
were the evening's entertainment?
It still can be.

Remember when a gentleman held the door for a
lady? Some still do.

Remember when kindness was not considered heroic
but was just what you extended?
It still is.

Remember when parents taught their children
to be well groomed?
A few still do.

Remember when humility was a valued
characteristic in human beings?
It still is.

Remember when playing in a field with animals
and nature was more valued than television?
It still is.

PATHWAYS TO LOVE

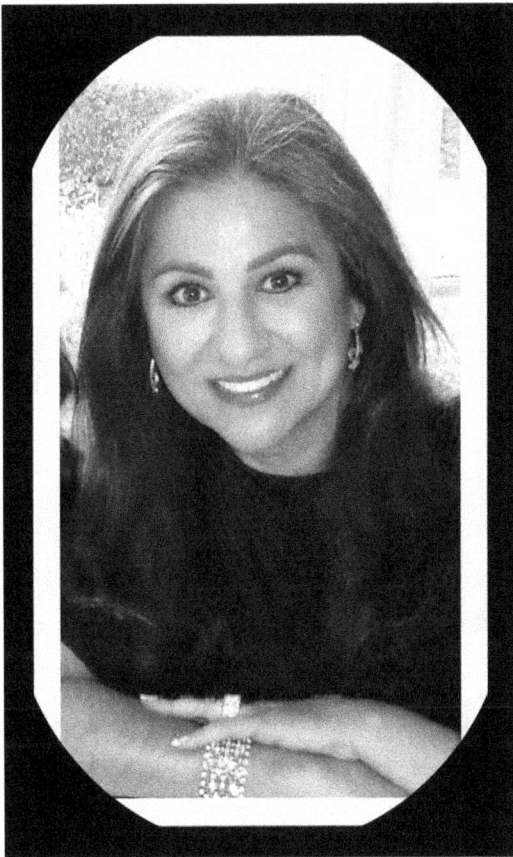

The Sacred Art of Language

Words are only the vehicle for energy and intention yet when formulated with love they can alter your very DNA. They have the power to injure and destroy or uplift and inspire. Use words as if every word which springs from your lips either increases or decreases your bank account, because you are actually doing just that. You can increase the quality and magnitude of your light, your frequency, your health and vastly improve the quality of your relationships or you can grow spiritually bankrupt with the misuse of language.

Science has studied the effects of words on the biological composition of the human being and the results have been startling. In his book "Hidden Messages in Water" Dr. Masaru Emoto has shown the effects words have on water and when you realize that the human body is comprise of up to 60% water you begin to understand the importance of your daily use of language.

My wish for you is that you embrace the power of intention and wield a positive dialogue with others and of course within yourself. My hope is that you know how powerful you are and are becoming each day you practice using a deliberate dialogue which transforms the world around you as you embrace loving and serving others. The earth is full of goodness and despite all we see around us which defies that notion, I choose to embrace the transformational power of love while stepping into its all engulfing abyss where energy dances in fields of light and is fed from the infinite stream the entire universe was built upon. May your journey take you to the pristine paradise which exists right here on earth; a world where life flows at the perfect pace, where the colors of mother earth and nature feed the soul and where joy and happiness are not only a divine right but are essential to a life fulfilled. May you know the shear elation of dancing barefoot in the rain, of lying in a field of brilliantly colored wildflowers staring up at an azure blue sky filled with white billowing clouds. May you just once, know what it's like for a wild, untamed animal to feed from your hand without feeling a moment of fear; may you visit a third world country and intertwine with those who live at the opposite polarity. May you walk through an emerald green forest and find yourself hugging a soft, fern crusted tree or taste the purity of the woodsy earth as you drink from an alpine stream. I hope that you learn to be alone with yourself feeling pure contentment as you ponder the mysteries of the universe and visit kingdoms you can only see with your eyes closed. My hope is that you learn to hone your awareness, that it may extend far beyond the earthly into the other worlds where the magic awaits you, the spiritual scholars who've come to change the world.

With Beams of Love, Light and Laughter,
Ariaa

Thank you for purchasing "The Book of Ariaa ~ Quotes for a Luminous Life".

I hope you enjoyed reading it and look forward to hearing from you personally. I would deeply appreciate it if you would write an honest review of this book and how it impacted you or what you gained from reading it at the following link.

http://www.amazon.com/TheBookofAriaa

If you would like to contact me, I would be delighted to hear from you. If you would like to book an appointment with me feel free to visit my website and click on "Book a session with Ariaa".

Wishing all of you blessings on your journey to enlightenment and joy.

Whatever you do, wherever you are and whatever you become, please remember to use your heart and soul to LOVE OUTLOUD!

With Beams of Love, Light and Laughter,
Ariaa Jaeger

Website: http://Ariaa.com

To book Ariaa for personal appearances, television or radio guest appearances, spiritual gatherings, lectures and public speaking venues, voiceovers or vocal performances, you may contact Ariaa directly. Her current contact information can be found on her website.

Facebook:
https://www.facebook.com/AriaaJaeger?ref=tn_tnmn

Facebook page:
https://www.facebook.com/BeamsOfLove

Facebook music page:
https://www.facebook.com/AriaaTunes?ref=hl

Twitter:
https://twitter.com/AriaaJaeger

Google+:
https://plus.google.com/107140978127037205310/posts

LinkedIn:
http://www.linkedin.com/profile/
view?id=25696735&trk=nav_responsive_tab_profilec

Other books by Ariaa Jaeger:
"Ariaaisms ~ Spiritual Food for the Soul"
ISBN: 978-0-9895503-8-3 (sc)
ISBN: 978-0-9895503-3-8 (e)
Printed in the United States of America
Released September 2013

www.ingramcontent.com/pod-product-compliance
Lightning Source LLC
Chambersburg PA
CBHW051953090426
42741CB00008B/1369